D1279397

DRUGS AND LOW SELF-ESTEEM

A person with low self-esteem has trouble taking pride in his or her accomplishments.

THE DRUG ABUSE PREVENTION LIBRARY

DRUGS AND LOW SELF-ESTEEM

Kenneth R. Shepherd

THE ROSEN PUBLISHING GROUP, INC.

NEW YORK

for my wife, Kala

The people pictured in this book are only models. They in no way practice or endorse the activities illustrated. Captions serve only to explain the subjects of photographs and do not in any way imply a connection between the real-life models and the staged situations.

Published in 1998 by The Rosen Publishing Group, Inc.
29 East 21st Street, New York, NY 10010

Library of Congress Cataloging-in-Publication Data
Shepherd, Kenneth R.
 Drugs and low self-esteem / Kenneth R. Shepherd.
 p. cm. -- (The drug abuse prevention library)
 Includes bibliographical references and index.
 Summary: Discusses various aspects of low self-esteem, how it can lead to drug abuse, the negative consequences, and where to get help for such a problem.
 ISBN 0-8239-2826-8
 1. Teenagers—Drug use—United States—Juvenile literature. 2. Drug abuse—United States—Juvenile literature. 3. Self-esteem in adolescence—United States—Juvenile literature. [1. Drug abuse. 2. Self-esteem.] I. Title. II. Series.
 HV5824.Y68S525 1998
 616.86'071'0835—dc21   98-8497
                                                    CIP
                                                    AC

Manufactured in the United States of America

Contents

Introduction

*H*ow would you answer these questions?

Do you like yourself?
Do you think that you're good enough to compete with others?
Do you think you're in charge of your life?

How did you answer these questions? If you answered "No" to all of them, you may have low self-esteem. If so, you're not alone. Many people think of themselves as not very likable, not very good, and not very important. They don't believe in themselves, and they feel that their lives aren't under their control.

How do you feel about your life? Do other people seem to enjoy themselves more than you do? How do you feel when

People may use drugs to escape feelings of sadness.

8 you have finished something you have been working on for a long time—satisfied and proud of yourself, or dissatisfied and unhappy? The thoughts and feelings you have about yourself and your life are what make up your self-esteem.

Self-esteem is more than just a way of measuring the things you've accomplished. It has a lot to do with attitude—the way you approach a problem or a situation. Self-esteem also influences your feelings. A person with good self-esteem will feel good about him or herself; a person with low self-esteem will generally feel bad about his or her accomplishments.

Low self-esteem comes from many sources, both outside and inside of yourself. If other people treat you poorly, you may start to treat yourself poorly. Low self-esteem also has many consequences: you shy away from trying new things and from expressing how you feel. But feelings are powerful. People who feel unable to express emotions sometimes turn to drugs instead to try to escape their feelings.

Using drugs may seem like a way to fit in with people, boost self-confidence, and improve self-esteem. But the reality of drug use is very different. It can lead to drug abuse and addiction—which can cause you to become even more anxious and with-drawn from others. Instead of solving your problems, drug abuse creates new prob-lems. The only way to improve self-esteem is to understand the causes of it, and to make a positive effort toward change.

This book discusses how to recognize if you have low self-esteem. It shows how low self-esteem can lead to drug abuse, and how drug abuse can reinforce feelings of low self-esteem. It explores what you can do to build your self-confidence, and where you can get the help and support you need.

Your attitude on the job, at school, and at home is affected by your self-esteem.

CHAPTER 1

Self-Esteem and You

Geoffrey can't figure Margaret out. She rarely talks to people and never looks them in the face when she does. He's been in the same class with her for three years, but he doesn't really know her. He even went with her on a coffee date, but she just sat at the table and stared into her coffee mug like she could see the future in it. She doesn't answer when he says "Hello." Geoffrey still likes her, but he doesn't understand why she acts the way she does.

Caleb works long hours as a cashier in a fast-food restaurant. He isn't thrilled with the job, but he wants to make enough money to buy a good car and pay his tuition to the local community college. He figures that education and transportation will help make his future a lot brighter.

12 *Caleb tries to make his job more bearable by being friendly to customers. He has found that it makes the time go by quickly. Recently he received a raise of twenty-five cents an hour, and the manager wants him to attend a management training program the company offers. Caleb doesn't want to stay at this job forever, but management training would look very good on a résumé.*

Attitude. People use the word *attitude* to mean a lot of different things. Rap stars have an "attitude." If you disagree with a teacher, or talk back to your father, you can be accused of having "a bad attitude." Although no one defines exactly what attitude is, you can usually recognize it when you see or hear it.

Margaret seems distant from others, but the reason is that she has a bad attitude toward herself. On the other hand, Caleb has a more positive outlook. What makes this difference?

The Difference
Overall, people who have a positive view of themselves

- are less likely to get stressed out over the inevitable bumps in life;

If you have a positive view of yourself, you will value and trust your opinions and ideas.

- value and trust their own ideas and opinions;
- are psyched to try new things;
- feel comfortable giving and accepting compliments; and
- speak up when something is bothering them.

People with low self-esteem don't feel as secure. They:

- feel misunderstood;
- are afraid of failure;
- don't try new things;
- have trouble pinpointing and expressing how they feel;

14

- think their ideas aren't important; and
- prefer being alone to being with others.

There are many things that contribute to low self-esteem. The environment you grew up in is an important factor. Another one is your self-talk—the the conversations you have with yourself as things happen to you.

Looking at Your Environment

You are a product of your environment (the world around you). That includes your family, your friends, and your society. The people around you help you become who you are—they teach you values, and help you develop your self-image.

The people around you can make a big difference in your life. They can help you have positive experiences and expect success by encouraging you and praising your progress. Or they can tell you that you are worthless and that you will fail by discouraging you and saying, "you're an idiot," "you're hopeless," and "can't you do anything right?" Having negative experiences can take a heavy toll on your self-esteem.

If people tell you negative things about yourself, you may start to believe them.

Family Problems

Scott was sick of the way his mother and father behaved. They argued constantly. His father was a house painter but he spent most of his time sitting around the house watching television, or in the garage working on his motorcycle instead of looking for work.

Scott's mother was the breadwinner. She liked to invite people over to visit—often people from her workplace that she didn't know very well. She demanded a spotless house and yard in order to impress her guests. She insisted that the grass be kept cut, the garden weeded weekly, and the house swept and dusted every day. She expected Scott's father to do these chores when he wasn't working, but he didn't. Scott ended up doing the chores to keep his mother from getting angry.

16   *When Scott got a job delivering refrigerators at a local appliance dealership, though, he had to stop covering for his father. The chores didn't get done.*

The first time Scott's mother came home and found the chores undone, she became very upset. She screamed at Scott and his father. Finally she got so angry that she picked up a vase from the mantel and threw it at them.

Whenever his parents fought, Scott usually went to his room and stayed there until the house was quiet again. This time, though, he left the house and went into the garage. He felt responsible for not doing the chores. He saw his father's motorcycle in the corner. Maybe there was someplace he could go where he wouldn't have to deal with his parents.

Scott got on the cycle and reached for the helmet. The next instant, he went roaring down the driveway and into the night.

Unfortunately, it's common for teens to grow up in unhappy homes. With almost half of marriages ending in divorce, many teens witness fighting between their parents. Even in the best circumstances—when your parents let you know that their problems aren't your fault and that they love you—it's easy to feel that your parents' problems are your problems. That can feel overwhelming.

Many teens don't even feel secure. If |
you live in poverty, surrounded by crime and drug abuse, you may feel that you have a slim chance to succeed in life. Or your parents just may not give you the guidance that you need. All of these things put a lot of stress on you as you're growing up.

Scott's problem was rooted in his family situation. He was angry and frustrated with the way his parents were behaving. He felt trapped between his mother's anger and his father's neglect. Scott didn't think that there was anything he could do about his situation.

As a consequence, the situation affected how Scott thought about himself. He learned that doing things for himself (such as taking a job) was a negative move, not a positive one. When a conflict came up, Scott felt that he couldn't work things out with his parents, or confide in anyone.

Fitting In

Rochelle has just started tenth grade. Last year, when she was a freshman, she pulled As and Bs. She had been able to breeze through her homework in less than an hour. This year her grades were not as good. She felt confused by the assignments—she was spending two or three hours a night on homework, and the work was still wrong.

Fitting in is important to everyone.

The biggest problem Rochelle had, though, was feeling lonely. She had some acquaintances, but no real friends. No one seemed to be making an effort to stay friends with her, either. She worried that she didn't belong and worried that she might never fit in.

At times the loneliness felt like a big hand squeezing her heart. Sometimes the pain was so bad that she couldn't pay attention in class. It even kept her awake at night.

Everyone wants to feel accepted. Fitting in is very important to teens. Hanging out with a group helps you define who you are, apart from your family. Friends help lift you up when you are feeling down.

The flip side is that when you don't fit in, or when your group of friends changes,

it hurts. Sometimes it's easy to believe that | **19**
it's your fault—that you did something
wrong, or that no one will ever like you. It
may feel that way sometimes. But if you
develop a positive attitude, you will feel
better about yourself and others—and that
will change how others view you, too.

Stress from a Change in Life

*Karin had been one of the most attractive
girls in high school. The whole varsity football
squad had tried to date her when she was a
junior. Senior year, she was elected homecom-
ing queen.*

*But after graduation, Karin's life took a
sharp turn. She hadn't applied to colleges
until very late—she was wait-listed at two of
them, and rejected from the other three. Her
parents suggested she enroll at community
college for the first year. But Karin was losing
interest in school. She worked three days a
week at a boutique, and was getting bored
with her job too. She avoided her friends who
seemed to spend all their time talking about
going away to school.*

*Karin started to spend more and more time
alone at home. She turned to eating as a way
to comfort herself. Karin had never stressed out
about gaining weight; but as she put on
seventy pounds over the next seven months,*

20 | *Karin felt even worse about herself. She hardly ever went out of the house—especially when her friends were home on break from school.*

Karin's problem was rooted in her own self-image. She felt attractive and desirable while she was in high school. Her self-esteem started to suffer when she graduated and grew distant from her friends. Karin dealt with her problems by turning to food: as long as she was eating, she didn't have to think about her feelings.

Your self-esteem can take a blow when you are confronted by change and transition in your life. You're under stress, facing a completely new situation. Periods of change are when self-destructive behaviors, such as eating disorders and drug abuse, are more likely to take hold.

It's helpful to recognize the sources of low self-esteem because once you do, you can see more clearly how they affect you, and how you can counter them. One key way is to examine your "self-talk."

Self-Talk: What We Think Is What We Become

The attitude you have toward your life—work, school, family, friends—determines how you react and how you feel when you

Low self-esteem can be a major cause of an eating disorder.

22 | reach a stressful point in your life. You atti-
tude forms from your environment: the
family you grew up in, your friends, and the
other people you know.

You probably began forming your attitude early in your life. The process probably started so long ago that now you don't
even think about it.

One way you can understand your attitude toward life is to listen to your "self-
talk." Self-talk is really just that:
conversations that we have with ourselves. It
can be in the form of a private conversation
in our heads, or mental pictures and images,
or even words spoken out loud. Your self-
esteem gets reinforced through self-talk.

*Jennifer had a hard time understanding
what the teacher wanted her to write for her
English term paper. She felt stupid for not understanding the assignment and felt too timid to ask
the teacher to explain it more clearly. She ended
up paraphrasing material from a library book.
When she turned it in, she wasn't proud of the
job she had done. When she got the paper back,
it was marked C minus.*

How would you react to this situation?
Self-talk plays a big part, because what
you think affects what you do.

Positive Self-Talk	Negative Self-Talk	*23*
I didn't do my best.	I'm such an idiot.	
Why didn't I get it?	I'll never get it.	
I should have asked Mr. Velazquez for a clearer explanation of what he wanted.	Mr. Velazquez is out to get me.	
I've got to put more time into the next assignment.	I'm dropping this dumb class.	

A person with positive self-talk would view this as a learning experience. A person with negative self-talk might just give up, reinforcing the idea that she "just can't do it."

Your self-talk is what makes you feel able to make decisions and change things, or unable to do so. This is especially true when you encounter setbacks. With negative self-talk, you tend to criticize yourself ("I'm such an idiot") and get stressed out. And when you're stressed, it's easy to spread the blame onto other people too ("Mr. Velazquez is out to get me") and dodge the situation ("I'm dropping this dumb class"). These are defenses that, in some ways, protect you from feeling hurt. But they don't always have the best effect

24 on you—you're putting yourself down and feeling that the situation is beyond your control.

Positive self-talk, on the other hand, helps keep things in perspective. Although something happened that wasn't perfect, you are able to look at what went wrong without beating up on yourself. What's more, you will have learned how to handle the situation better next time.

Later in this book you'll find out how to change your self-talk and improve your self-esteem.

CHAPTER 2

The Beginnings of Drug Use

*W*hen Donna's father got a new job, her family moved. Donna had always been shy, and she had a hard time making new friends. She felt that no one wanted to talk to her. Guys acted like they didn't see her at all. Sometimes she saw other girls looking at her, and she felt that they were making fun of her. Every day Donna walked home alone rather than take the bus with all the people on it. She was very lonely, but she felt that being alone was less painful than being around people who didn't like her.

Things were going badly at home, too. Her mom got laid off from her job. Her dad was working two jobs and always came home tired. Sometimes late at night Donna could hear her parents arguing about money. Sometimes they

25

People often turn to drugs as a social crutch or to ease anxieties about themselves.

fought about Donna, too. When she brought *home a poor grade from school, her father threw a fit. "Can't you do anything right?" he yelled.*

No one seemed to have much time for her. Donna's old boyfriend, Nate, didn't call her anymore. She thought about calling him, but she thought that he'd probably found a new girlfriend. It would just be embarrassing.

Then there was Jake. Jake wore cool clothes. He was popular. A party wasn't a party unless Jake was there.

Jake started paying attention to Donna. He smiled at her whenever he saw her. He stopped in the halls to talk to her. Then one day he asked her to go to a party. When they got there, Jake and some of his friends went to get some beer.

Jake handed Donna a beer. She didn't like the taste much, but she liked the way it made her feel. When she was drinking, her bad feelings about herself weren't as strong. It seemed easier to talk to other people. She forgot about her problems at home.

Donna started going to parties and drank five or six beers at every party. Sometimes, late at night when her parents were in bed, she drank some of her dad's beer. Soon she spent most of her time thinking about when she could sneak her next drink.

28 Like many teens, Donna wanted to be part of the "in" crowd at her school. She wanted to have friends and be popular. But her poor confidence and low self-esteem, and the trouble she experienced at home, made it hard for her to make friends. She felt lonely.

Because Donna told herself she was worthless, she saw herself as a victim of a situation she couldn't control. She didn't try to change her life—she just became unhappy and felt she was doomed to be unpopular.

Drugs and Their Effects

Like Donna, people with low self-esteem may turn to drugs as a social crutch, or to ease anxieties about themselves. This is because drugs can make you feel powerful, relaxed, and less inhibited. But even though drugs may temporarily make a person feel more confident, drugs only mask the problem of having low self-esteem. They don't solve it.

At the same time, drugs seriously damage how your body functions and how your mind works. These effects differ from drug to drug.

- *Depressants:* Alcohol, heroin, China White, Special K. Depressants slow down your body functions, such as

Drugs can seriously damage how your body functions and how your mind works.

breathing and heart rate. They harm your ability to perceive the world around you and cause long-term damage to your liver and kidneys. If you inject heroin, you are also at high risk for contracting HIV from unsterilized needles.

- *Hallucinogens:* Marijuana, hashish, LSD, peyote, magic mushrooms, mescaline, PCP (angel dust), and Ecstasy. A "trip" on one of these drugs causes you to have hallucinations—see and feel things that aren't really there. They can cause permanent brain damage.
- *Amphetamines:* Amphetamines (speed), methamphetamine (ice,

30 crystal meth, crank). These are synthetic (human-made) drugs that speed up your mind and body. They can cause permanent heart and brain damage.

- *Inhalants:* Household products containing solvents that are inhaled, producing a "head rush" or "high." They can cause organ damage and even instant death.
- *Cocaine and crack:* These drugs, which come from the coca plant, produce a very intense rush and speed up your nervous system. They are highly addictive, and damage your heart and brain.

Why Take Drugs?

Why do people start using drugs? It may be a combination of factors.

- *Fitting in:* Almost all people want others to notice and accept them. Sometimes that means feeling that you have to go along with the crowd. Even if you don't want to, you may be pressured to experiment with drugs. Teens often start out using marijuana and alcohol, and then start using drugs such as

cocaine, amphetamines, and heroin.
- *Growing up with drugs:* You can also learn to use drugs from your environment. If your parents drink or take drugs, it's easy to believe that it's okay. If your brother or sister uses drugs, you may want to be like him or her.
- *Escaping problems:* People in an unhappy home or work life may think drugs will provide temporary relief from feelings of frustration. The problem is that when the drugs wear off, the feelings are still there—drugs have only worsened the situation.

Many people who turn to drugs aren't fully aware of all the harm they do.

A person who has high self-esteem is less likely to do something that will hurt him or her. By learning to value yourself for being the person you are and by educating yourself about the dangers of drugs, you can keep yourself from falling into the trap of drug abuse.

A drug high is followed by a crash, with unpleasant side effects such as headache, dehydration, and irritability.

CHAPTER 3

The Consequences of Drug Use

*J*orge had a lot of friends. He did well in school and had a good part-time job. He played on the second-string basketball team. He was getting along well with his girlfriend, Kara. People liked to have him around.

Then one night a friend asked him if he and Kara wanted to hang out at a dance club. Jorge said okay. The people there were friendly. The music was terrific, and he and Kara danced the night away. They didn't get home until three o'clock in the morning.

Then one night one of the guys at the club introduced them to a drug called Ecstasy. Kara didn't want to try it, but Jorge did. It seemed to make all his feelings more intense. The music and the lights seemed even more inviting. Everyone he met seemed to be his friend.

34 *When the high wore off, though, Jorge crashed. He was very thirsty and felt awful. He was in a bad mood when he woke up. He didn't get up until early afternoon that day. The next weekend, he went to the club and used Ecstasy again. He had a fabulous time again. But when the drug began to wear off, he didn't want to come down. He bought some more. When that wore off, he felt even more horrible.*

Soon Jorge was trapped in a cycle of ups and downs. He went to the club on the weekends and then felt low for a part of each week. His grades dropped. He was cranky at work, which hurt his performance. He was benched for missing too many basketball practices. Kara noticed these changes and told him she was concerned. Jorge said he was okay, he could handle it. Later, when she expressed concern again, he blew her off. Soon after, she broke up with him.

Jorge knew that his life was slipping out of control. But he still was craving the next high from Ecstasy.

Drugs are so powerful, and have such a strong effect on users, it's easy to slip into a pattern of abuse. Many teens start using drugs only once in a while. But soon, they start using more and more often.

Drugs create two different kinds of effects on users: psychological dependence and physical dependence. Psychological dependence is when you crave the emotional effects that a drug gives you— often an escape from problems or stress in your life.

David's mom kept a bottle of vodka in the refrigerator—"to help her sleep," she said. David began sneaking downstairs after his mother went to bed and drinking shots of vodka. At first he did it just for fun. But he also found that the vodka made him feel more relaxed, and it let him forget about not making the basketball team. After a while he began drinking shots right after school. A little later he began skipping his last class just so he could get home early, open the refrigerator, and pull out the bottle.

Physical dependence is when your body begins to crave the drug. This happens when you use the drug regularly and develop a tolerance to its effects. that means that you need to take more and more of the drug in order to get the same high.

A drug high is always followed by a "crash"—a feeling of coming down. You feel unpleasant side effects, such as

35

If you plan your life around getting drunk or high, you may have a problem with drugs.

headache, dry mouth, and irritability. If you are addicted to a drug, you may also feel a strong need to use the drug again. When a person becomes physically dependent on a drug and then stops using it, the user experiences a painful withdrawal.

Rochelle was scared. She and her boyfriend Timi had been using cocaine together for weeks now. At first she enjoyed the sensations the drug gave her. It made her feel more alive and happier than usual. But about an hour later, when the drug wore off, she often felt worse than before. And the depression she felt continued until she took more cocaine. Even worse, the more she used the drug, the less effect it had on her. Soon she was taking cocaine just to feel normal. When she tried to stop, the feelings of anxiety and depression overwhelmed her.

The Stages of Addiction

Virtually no one who uses drugs ever thinks he or she will become addicted to them. A person usually goes through three steps in the process of becoming addicted.

Experimentation

Keli had never tried beer before her sophomore year in high school. Her friends urged her

38   *to drink with them. "How will you know if you like it if you don't try it?" they asked.*

Keli wasn't so sure. She knew that alcohol screwed up the body and made her friends act weird. But she wanted to see what it was like. Her friends seemed happy when they were drunk—kind of relaxed and silly. She didn't want to look lame in front of them.

In the experimentation stage, a teen is curious about drugs. She might even try one or more different drugs. Usually, this happens in social situations—at parties or clubs.

Many people believe that taking drugs occasionally isn't a problem. They believe that they are in control of their lives and can handle a shot or a joint every now and then. But any drug—even a drug as common as alcohol and even if it is taken in small amounts—distorts their judgment and their reasoning powers. Some drugs, such as crack, can be addictive the first time a person tries it.

Regular use

Fred was shy, but with his friend Tom he started partying every weekend. He liked alcohol and pot, but after a while, used only cocaine. During the week he would daydream

about getting high. He thought he needed it to **39**
improve his personality.

*Fred stopped seeing many of his old buddies
and hung out only with his drug-using friends.
His old friends were worried about him. They
knew that he used drugs and were afraid that
he could be in trouble. "I'm all right—don't
worry about me," he told them. "I can give it
up whenever I want to."*

In this stage, a person starts to change
his lifestyle around his drug habit. He or
she may narrow down to using only one
drug. Drug use has started to interfere with
relationships with others.

If confronted, the user will insist that it's
no big deal, that everything is under
control. But the reality is that he's on the
road to addiction.

Addiction

*Michael started showing up high at school
and work. Then he stopped showing up at all.
His parents knew he came and went at all
hours, but had no idea what to do about it.*

*Michael ran out of money to pay for drugs.
So he started stealing. First he stole from his
parents' wallets. Then he and his drug-using
friends started breaking into houses and stealing any valuables they could find.*

People addicted to drugs may steal from their families in order to get money for drugs.

Michael's parents couldn't take it **41**
anymore. They threw him out of the house.
They said they were sick of his lying about
"not having a problem." Michael started
living on the street and begging for change.

Addiction is often the nightmare result
of drug use. The addict's mind and body
are dependent on the drug. He or she will
do anything to get it—including lie and
steal from his or her own family. At the
same time, the addict will deny that he or
she has a problem, even if his or her life and
health are in jeopardy.

Addiction can happen very quickly. This
is especially true for teens, whose bodies
and minds are still developing. For
instance, studies have shown that it can
take several years for an older person's
pattern of alcohol abuse to result in addiction, but a teenager can become addicted
to alcohol in less than a year.

Consequences of Drug Addiction

There are many serious consequences of
drug addiction—no matter what your
reasons for turning to drugs. The boost to
self-esteem and confidence that you feel is
only temporary: after a while, the effects of
the drug wear off.

Overdosing can lead to critical or deadly situations.

As you develop a tolerance to a drug—need more and more of it in order to get the same high—you put yourself at higher risk for overdose. You may crave a quantity of drugs that your system can't handle.

Kristi knew that Steven, her boyfriend, had used cocaine last year. He had told her that he didn't use it anymore. But when Steven started acting strange and nervous all the time, Kristi suspected that he had started getting high again.

Kristi tried to confront Steven. But nothing she said seemed to have any effect on him. "Don't worry about me," he said. "I can take it. It doesn't affect me." By their junior year he stopped coming to school. Sometimes Kristi would come over to his place on Saturday mornings and find him still passed out from partying on Friday night. One day she came and found him lying on the floor. He wasn't breathing. She ran to the telephone and called 911. The paramedics later told her that Steven had died of an overdose.

Depression can be another result of drug abuse. Depression is more severe than feeling "blue" or "down in the dumps." It is an illness that makes it hard to function on a day-to-day basis. A depressed person:

- has overwhelming feelings of sadness;
- loses interest in activities;
- has difficulty concentrating;
- has sleep problems;
- feels guilty or worthless much of the time.

Sometimes people take drugs in order to avoid depression. But this can be very dangerous. Depressants ("downers") actually increase symptoms of depression. Some people take stimulants ("uppers") thinking that they can ease symptoms of depression. But the crash that they experience can actually make their depression worse.

Counseling—in groups or one-on-one—is helpful for teens who are overcoming drug problems.

Muhammad had not seen his father since he was very young. His mother was a crack addict. He was placed in a group foster home when he turned fourteen, where he lived with fifteen other boys his age. The foster home workers were nice enough, but he didn't feel that any of them really cared about him.

Muhammad started using speed when he was at the foster home. He felt it was a good "pick up" when he felt lonely and hopeless. But his feelings of hopelessness were getting even worse. Some days he felt he couldn't get out of bed in the morning.

One evening after using drugs, Muhammad felt himself starting to crash. Only he was too tired to take more speed. All he wanted to do was die.

About 60 percent of all teenagers who commit suicide suffer from drug abuse. This trend continues even among older drug users. Over 15 percent of alcoholics of all ages eventually commit suicide. These statistics are scary. But there is hope.

Recovery

People who are addicted to alcohol, heroin, or other drugs are in serious danger. But it is possible to recover. Recovery can take many painful weeks or months, but it will save your life.

If you or someone you know is struggling with a drug problem and is ready to do something about it, the most important thing to do is find help. Talk to any responsible adult that you trust. A parent, brother, or sister, a teacher, a family doctor, or a clergyman are all ideal.

If for some reason you don't feel comfortable approaching someone you know, you can check the Yellow Pages under Drug Abuse Counseling and Social Service Organizations for help. The important thing is to get some assistance now.

Many treatment options are open to you. They include:

• Inpatient treatment: a live-in situation that keeps you safe while you are

46 withdrawing from drugs. This could be at a hospital or clinic. Many clinics are free.

- Twelve-Step programs: meetings held by other recovering drug abusers who share their experiences. The Twelve Steps are a series of principles of spiritual self-discovery. By "working" the steps, you develop a support system in living a drug-free life. Twelve-Step programs are free.
- Therapy: meetings with a therapist (a trained professional in the mental health field). These meetings may be one-on-one, with your family, or in a group of other recovering drug abusers. If you or your parents have medical insurance, ask your insurance company about their coverage.

The good news is that, even though no one can improve your low self-esteem but you, many qualified professionals can help you develop a healthier self-esteem. They can assist you in resolving problems stemming from your lack of self-esteem. With the right support, you can become the person you want to be.

CHAPTER 4

Boosting Self-Esteem

If you or someone you care about has low self-esteem, he or she may be at risk for drug abuse. But it possible to improve your self-esteem.

People with high self-esteem like themselves. They feel confident in their abilities and accept their strengths and weaknesses. They are less likely than others to feel the need to use drugs to try to improve their mood.

People with low self-esteem, on the other hand, usually don't like themselves. They think things like, "Nobody likes me," "I'm not good at anything," or "I'm a failure." They do this because they have fallen into a habit of negative self-talk.

47

48   *Charles has always loved basketball, but he never felt that he was very good at it. When he misses a basket he tells himself, "I should have had that. I'm just no good at this." He expects to miss the baskets, and whenever he does he says, "I knew that would happen. I'm an idiot. I can't even do the thing I love most right."*

The good news is that self-talk is completely reversible. A person can go from a poor self-image and low self-esteem to a good self-image and high self-esteem. More good news: it's a fairly simple process. However, it is not an easy trip. No one can do it for you, although lots of people can and will help you on the way. The important thing for you to do is start now. And don't stop.

Identifying Real Fears

There are a lot of things in life that can threaten us. Fear is useful as a survival trait: it can keep us out of life-threatening situations. For example, most people have a fear of heights. That makes them stop and think twice before walking along a dangerously high cliff.

But it's important to remember that the fears that contribute to low self-esteem

You can boost your self-esteem by trying something new.

aren't based on present danger. Instead, they're based on negative experiences in the past.

One way you can overcome these negative experiences is to take risks. That may mean trying new things—sports, music, asking someone out on a date.

Sometimes when you try something new, you don't succeed. But your attitude can make the difference between success and failure. If you believe that you'll lose, you'll lose. But if you believe you'll win, you'll win.

Jeanette is training for the newly organized women's hockey team at school. She gets a lot of negative feedback from people who think

50 | *hockey is a man's game and believe that women shouldn't play it. But Jeanette knows she's good at it. When someone criticizes her for learning to play hockey, she lets it roll off her back. She's getting better at hockey every day.*

It's pretty easy to tell the difference between a losing mentality and a winning mentality. A loser is paralyzed by fear—fear of life, and fear of taking action. A loser gives up easily. Most of all, a loser expects to fail.

So how can you change your attitude from a loser to a winner? A winner does not give up. A winner is not reckless, but is not afraid. A winner is not a victim of circumstances because a winner controls his or her own life.

Using Positive Thinking

One of the most important things you can do about low self-esteem is to learn to think positively. A negative attitude, more than anything else, can contribute to a loss of self-esteem. Why defeat yourself with a negative attitude?

Tamara likes to sing. She wants to audition for the small ensemble group at school. But the ensemble group, which sings special music and tours all around the state, requires its members to memorize the music they perform. Memorization scares Tamara. But she tells herself, "This is not that hard. I can do this." When the time comes for her audition, she passes the test easily.

Here are some things you can do to help boost your own self-image and your positive thinking.

1. Make a list of all your best traits. Start each line with the phrase, "I'm really good at . . ." Put the list up where you'll see it every day—next to your bed or on your mirror. Add to it every time you succeed at something.

2. Set realistic goals. If you have a major objective, break it down into a series of steps. Instead of aiming at one big, difficult goal, plan the steps that it will take to get you there. Then work on the steps one by one. Ask a school counselor, teacher, or parent to help you figure out what steps are needed to achieve your goal.

3. Make time for yourself. Put aside part of every day just to do the things you like to do. If you pay attention to your needs

Making a list of your best traits can help boost your self-image
and positive thinking.

on a regular basis, you'll grow to like yourself better and your self-esteem will soar.

Changing Self-Talk

You can raise your self-esteem by changing
your self-talk.

Listen to your thoughts. Imagine that
you're tape-recording them as you think
them; then play them back. Identify the
messages you're sending yourself. If you're
sending negative messages—such as "I'll
never get it, I can't do it"—change the
script to "I can get it; I can do it." This may
take a lot of effort at first. But if you keep
doing it, soon it will come automatically.

Patience and Persistence

Success doesn't come overnight. It's easy
to get discouraged, but it's important to
keep trying. You may fail many times
before you win. But if you stop on the way,
if you give up and quit, you will never
reach your goals.

*Jaime is taking the exam to enter a techni-
cal school training course in electronics. He's
done some preparation for the test, but he still
feels very nervous about his chances. When he
gets his results back, he sees that he's failed—*

54 *but not by very much. He studies some more and tries again two weeks later. He fails again, but his score continues to improve. On the sixth try, Jaime passes the test and is able to enroll in the program.*

Above all, be proud of yourself. Take pride in what you can do. Give yourself credit for trying new and different things. Even if you don't succeed right away, you are trying. And that makes more difference than all the failures in the world.

Glossary

addiction When someone is physically and psychologically dependent on a drug.

amphetamines Human-made drugs that act on the body as stimulants.

depressants Drugs that slow down body functions, such as breathing and heart rate.

eating disorders When someone has emotional issues linked to food and eating that lead to physical and emotional problems.

hallucinogens Drugs that, when taken, bring on a halllucinogenic "trip."

inhalants Products that can be inhaled, producing a "high" or "head rush."

inpatient treatment A live-in situation that keeps you safe while you are withdrawing from drugs.

56 | **self-esteem** The way a person feels about him- or herself.

self-image The way we feel we are seen by others.

self-talk Conversations we have with ourselves.

stimulants Drugs that speed up the mind and body.

Where to Go for Help

Yellow Pages of Telephone Book
Drug Abuse, Counseling, Social Services
  Organizations

White Pages of Telephone Book
Community Services, Drug Abuse
  Hotline

School Counselors, School Nurse, Drug Education and Student Services

Hotlines

Covenant House Nine Line
(800) 999-9999

National Institute on Drug Abuse
(800) 662-HELP

Youth Crisis Hotline
(800) 448-4663

58 | ## *In the United States*

Al-Anon Family Group Headquarters
1600 Corporate Landing Parkway
Virginia Beach, VA 23456
(800) 344-2666
Web site: http://www.al-anon.org/

Alcoholics Anonymous
P.O. Box 459
Grand Central Station
New York, NY 10163
(212) 870-3400
e-mail: 76245-2153@compuserve.com
Web site: http://www.alcoholics-anonymous.org/

National Council on Alcoholism and
Drug Dependence
12 W. 21st St.
New York, NY 10010
(800) 622-2255
e-mail: national@NCADD.org
Web site://http://www.ncadd.org/

National Clearinghouse for Alcohol and
Drug Information (NCADI)
P.O. Box 2345
Rockville, MD 20852
(301) 468-2600
e-mail: info@prevline.health.org
Web site: http://www.health.org/

National Institute of Mental health   *59*
Office of Public Information
Room 7-99
5600 Fishers Lane
Rockville, MD 20857
(301) 443-4513
e-mail: nimhinfo@nih.gov

In Canada

**Alcohol and Drug Dependency Infor-
  mation and Counseling Services
  (ADDICS)**
247 1/2 Portage Avenue, #2
Winnipeg, Manitoba R3J ON6
(204) 942-4730

Alcoholics Anonymous, Toronto
#502 Intergroup Office
234 Eglington Avenue E
Toronto, ON M4P 1K5
Canada

Narcotics Anonymous, Ontario
World Service Office
150 Brittania Road East, Unit 21
Mississauga, ON L4Z 2A4
(416) 507-0100

For Further Reading

Bradshaw, John. *Healing the Shame That Binds*. Deerfield Beach, Fla.: Health Communications, Inc., 1988.

Glass, George. *Drugs and Fitting In.* New York: The Rosen Publishing Group, 1997.

Hastings, Jill M., and Marion H. Hyppo. *An Elephant in the Living Room*. Center City, Minn.: Hazelden, 1994.

Ignoffo, Matthew. *Everything You Need to Know About Self-Confidence*. New York: The Rosen Publishing Group, 1996.

Lee, Mary Price, and Richard S. Lee. *Drugs and Codependency*. New York: The Rosen Publishing Group, Rev. ed. 1998.

McKoy, Kathy, and Charles Wibbelsman, MD. *Life Happens: A Teenager's Guide to Friends, Failure, Sexuality. Love, Rejection,*

Addiction, Peer Pressure, Families, Loss, Depression, and Change. New York: Perigree, 1996.

Septien, Al. *Everything You Need to Know About Codepencency.* New York: The Rosen Publishing Group. Rev. ed. 1997.

Stoop, David. *Self Talk: Key to Personal Growth.* Old Tappan, N.J.: F. H. Revell, 1982.

Index

About The Author

Kenneth R. Shepherd teaches in the Social Science department at Henry Ford Community College in Dearborn, Michigan.

Photo Credits

Photos on pgs. 7, 15, 40, 44 by Ira Fox; pgs. 18, 21 by Pablo Maldonado; pp. 32, 49 by Ethan Zindler; All other photos by Les Mills.